MODERN ART MAYHEM

QED

Picture Researcher: Ruth Smith
Editor: Joanna McInerney
Designer: Victoria Kimonidou
and Jillian Williams

Copyright © QED Publishing 2016
First published in the UK in 2016 by
QED Publishing
Part of The Quarto Group
The Old Brewery
6 Blundell Street
London, N7 9BH

Quarto is the authority on a wide range of topics.

Quarto educates, entertains and enriches the lives of our readers—enthusiasts and lovers of hands-on living.

www.quartoknows.com

A catalogue record for this book is available from the British Library.

ISBN 978 1 78493 634 1

Printed in China

Picture credits

(t=top, b=bottom, l=left, r=right, c=centre, fc=front cover)

6, 37l © Laura Ford; Tate, London 2015, 7tr © Wayne Thiebaud/ DACS 2016, London/VAGA, New York 2016; Meringue Mix, 1999 (oil on panel), Thiebaud, Wayne (b.1920) / Private Collection / Bridgeman Images 7l © 2016 The Andy Warhol Foundation for the Visual Arts, Inc. / Artists Rights Society (ARS), New York and DACS 2016, London; Campbell's Soup Can, 1962 (screen print), Warhol, Andy (1928-87) / Saatchi Collection, London, UK / Bridgeman Images 7br The Art Archive / Musée d'Orsay Paris / Collection Dagli Orti 8, 21 Pipilotti Rist 'Cape Cod Chandelier' 25th Feb 2016, Courtesy the artist, Luhring Augustine and Hauser & Wirth; epa european pressphoto agency b.v. / Alamy Stock Photo 9tr The Art Archive / DeA Picture Library / V. Pirozzi Cezanne 9 The Art Archive / Suzuki Collection Tokyo / Superstock 9 © World History Archive / Alamy Stock Photo 9 meunierd / Shutterstock.com 11tcr, 37tl Universal Images Group/Getty Images 11cl © Lebrecht Music and Arts Photo Library / Alamy Stock Photo fcbl, 11bcr © GL Archive / Alamy Stock Photo fcl, 15,18, 23, 25, 30 39 The Art Archive / Nasjonal Galleriet Oslo 28b © Niday Picture Library / Alamy Stock Photo 16tr © 2016 The Andy Warhol Foundation for the Visual Arts, Inc. / Artists Rights Society (ARS), New York and DACS 2016, London; Nancy R. Schiff/Hulton Archive/ Getty Images fcr, 16bl © Burstein Collection/CORBIS 16bc © Succession Picasso/DACS, London 2016; The Art Archive / DeA Picture Library 16br The Guitar, illustration for the poem 'Au soleil du plafond', by Pierre Reverdy (1889-1960) 1955 (colour litho), Gris, Juan (1887-1927) / Bibliotheque Litteraire Jacques Doucet, Paris, France / Archives Charmet / Bridgeman Images 17 © The Pollock-Krasner Foundation ARS, NY and DACS, London 2016; The Art Archive / The Solomon R. Guggenheim Foundation / Art Resource, NY / Solomon R. Guggenheim Museum, New York. Gift, Janet C. Hauck, in loving memory of Alicia Guggenheim and Fred Hauck, 1991 17bt Art Archive/ 17bc The Art Archive / Musée Gustave Moreau Paris / Gianni Dagli Orti 17bb The

Art Archive / Brucke Museum Berlin 22 The Art Archive / Art Institute of Chicago 23 Alberto E. Rodriguez/WireImage/ Getty Images 26 © The Pollock-Krasner Foundation ARS, NY and DACS, London 2016; Martha Holmes/The LIFE Picture Collection/Getty Images fct, 27bl © Peter Horree / Alamy Stock Photo 27bc Art Archive/ 27br The House by the Railroad, 1925 (oil on canvas), Hopper, Edward (1882-1967) / Museum of Modern Art, New York, USA / Bridgeman Images 29 AC Manley / Shutterstock.com, 32r Concentric Circles, 1913 (oil on canvas), Kandinsky, Wassily (1866-1944) / Private Collection / Bridgeman Images 32c © Georg Baselitz 2016; Tate, London 2015 32l © The Pollock-Krasner Foundation ARS, NY and DACS, London 2016; The Museum of Modern Art, New York/Scala, Florence 33 Reflection (Self Portrait), 1985 (oil on canvas), Freud, Lucian (1922-2011) / Private Collection / © The Lucian Freud Archive / Bridgeman Images 34-35 Goldschmied & Chiari Where Shall We Go Dancing Tonight?, 2015, bottles, smoke, light, sound, confetti and Untitled View #44 and #45, 2015, digital print on mirror and glass, courtesy the artists and Museion Museum of Contemporary Art, Bozen, photo Museion 34 © Carl Andre/ Tate, London 2015 34r Trash_2006 - 2007_Gavin Turk_7199 (photographer Stephen White) 34t © Angela Verren Taunt. All rights reserved, DACS 2016; 1934 (relief - version 1), Nicholson, Ben (1894-1982) / Private Collection / James Austin / Bridgeman Images 36tr Fine Art Images/Heritage Images/Getty Images 37c Shutterstock/happydancing 37r Shutterstock/Villy Yovcheva 41tl © ADAGP, Paris and DACS, London 2016; The Art Archive / Musée d'Orsay Paris / Mondadori Portfolio/Electa 41c © Estate of Roy Lichtenstein/ DACS 2016; The Art Archive / Gianni Dagli Orti 41l © ADAGP, Paris and DACS, London 2016; The Art Archive / Musée d'Orsay Paris / Mondadori Portfolio/Electa 41r © ADAGP, Paris and DACS, London 2016; The Art Archive / Private Collection / Superstock

HOW TO BEGIN YOUR ADVENTURE

Are you ready for an amazing adventure in which you must outwit cunning enemies, stop villains trying to trick you, solve knotty puzzles and work out who is on your side? Then you've come to the right place!

Modern Art Mayhem isn't an ordinary book – you don't read the pages in order, 1, 2, 3... Instead you jump forwards and backwards through the book as you face a series of challenges. Sometimes you may lose your way, but keep your wits about you and the story will guide you back to where you need to be.

The story begins on page 4, and soon you'll find questions to answer and puzzles to solve. Choose the answers you think are correct and you'll see something like this:

If you think the correct answer is A

GO TO PAGE 37

If you think the correct answer is B

GO TO PAGE 13

If you think the correct answer is A, turn to page 37 and look for the same symbol in blue. That's where you'll find the next part of the story. If you make the wrong choice, the text will explain where you went wrong and let you have another go.

The problems in this book are about modern art. To solve them, you must use your knowledge of art and artists – and your common sense! To help you, there's a glossary of useful words at the back of the book, starting on page 44.

Are you ready?
Then turn the page and let your adventure begin!

MODERN ART MAYHEM...

You are doing summer work experience at Splosh Art Gallery. The phone rings one morning, waking you with a start. It's Cedric, the gallery owner.

"I've come down with a bug. I need your help with the finishing touches to the gallery before the Exhibition of the Year judges arrive — today!"

The gallery has won the competition for the last five years. The pressure is on you to make it amazing!

GET DRESSED AND **GET TO THE GALLERY** AS FAST AS YOU CAN ON PAGE 19

4

Yes, Edvard Munch used **tempera** (which is powdered **pigment** mixed with egg and water), as well as oil paints and **pastels** on cardboard.

Amazing! You're actually holding the world-famous painting! You ask security to put it in the main exhibition room. Suddenly you hear...

 MANAGER TO RECEPTION! IMMEDIATELY!

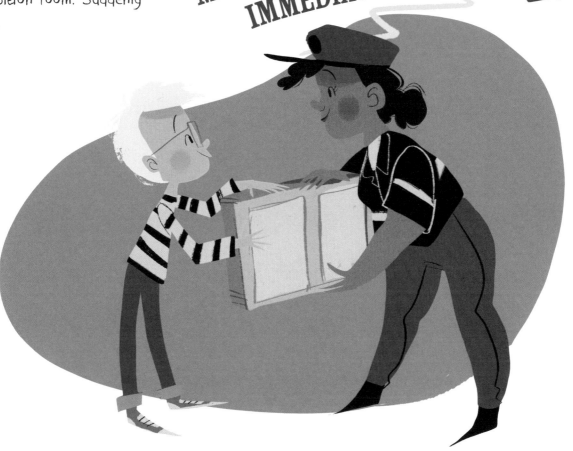

The judges must have arrived. Phew, you got everything ready just in time!

GO TO PAGE 29 TO **MEET THEM**

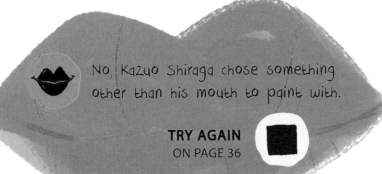 No, Kazuo Shiraga chose something other than his mouth to paint with.

TRY AGAIN ON PAGE 36

 No, **Naïve Art** looks simple, as if a child has made it. This is *Rhythme, Joie de vivre* by Robert Delaunay, painted in 1930. The style is called **Orphism**.

GO PACK TO PAGE 27 AND **TRY AGAIN** B

Yes! Laura Ford made *Moose*. It's bigger than life-size, made with metal, plaster, wool and fabric. She likes to give her animal sculptures human qualities.

You remember seeing the statue outside the gallery cafe. Quick, there's no time to lose!

You feel around and find an envelope tucked behind the antlers.

Laura Ford,
Moose, 1998

MENU

MENU

You open the next envelope
and read the note inside.

TODAY'S
SPECIALS

ROAST
LAMB
WITH
COUSCOUS
£14.50

Clue Three:
You're getting close,
soon you will applaud.
When you find my hideout,
behind the Wayne Thiebaud.

Which painting is the clue
referring to? What did
Wayne Thiebaud paint?

THE SOUP CAN.
CHECK ON PAGE 41

THE CAKES.
TURN TO PAGE 13

THE FRUIT.
LOOK ON PAGE 23

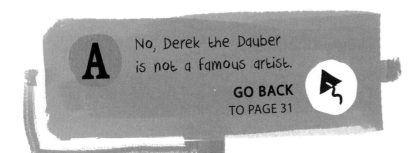

A No, Derek the Dauber is not a famous artist.

GO BACK
TO PAGE 31

No, Edvard Munch did not paint on canvas with oils.

GO BACK
TO PAGE 18

1

Yes, *Stepping Out* is a **Pop Art** painting by Roy Lichtenstein. You explain that Pop Art appeared in the 1950s and '60s and was about popular culture, such as magazines and film stars. Suddenly Don interrupts...

Hey, Andy. Tell the judges what the 'special' chandelier is made of.

Don smiles smugly. He's trying to make you look foolish.

Keep your cool. What do you say the chandelier is made out of?

THE FINEST CRYSTALS.
TURN TO PAGE 12

UNDERPANTS.
GO TO PAGE 21

VEGETABLES.
JUMP TO PAGE 33

Yes, works of art that depict everyday objects are called **still life**.

The judges seem impressed with you so far and Don looks cross, so you must be doing well!

Paul Cézanne, *Still Life with Basket*, 1888–90

Ah, but no Modern
Art exhibition is complete without
Pointillism. Do you have some?
My gallery does!

Everyone looks at you.
What do you say?

**WE HAVE A
POINTILLIST PAINTING
BY GEORGES SEURAT.**
GO TO PAGE 22

**YES, WE HAVE A WORK OF
ART BY BRIDGET RILEY.**
TURN TO PAGE 37

**YES, WE HAVE AN
ALEXANDER CALDER.**
GO TO PAGE 12

 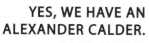 No, Lucian Freud didn't use black outlines!

HEAD BACK TO PAGE 33 AND
HAVE ANOTHER THINK

 Don't throw away the bin bag! Made of **bronze**, it's called *Trash*, and is by the artist Gavin Turk.

HAVE ANOTHER TRY
ON PAGE 35

Well done! Jonathan Borofsky made a number of these statues and put them in cities across the world in 1979.

The judges look impressed, until they spot a man in a strange costume dancing in the room next door!

What do you say to explain?

 IT'S FOR A CHILDREN'S PARTY IN THE CAFE.
TURN TO PAGE 42

 NOTHING! DON IS TRYING TO MAKE YOU LOOK STUPID. EEK!
GO TO PAGE 16

 HE'S DRESSED UP AS PERFORMANCE ART.
HEAD FOR PAGE 32

 No, *Adieu* by George Baselitz is the right way up!

TURN BACK TO PAGE 32 AND **TRY ONCE MORE**

 Vincent Van Gogh and Joan Miró famously painted the sun, but none of these pictures are part of the exhibition.

TRY AGAIN ON PAGE 19

C Yes! This painting is called *Wheatfield with Cypresses* by Vincent van Gogh.

The door unlocks and you step inside. It looks like someone has already been searching here. The room is a mess! You hope they didn't find anything.

You remember the second part of the clue:

Everyone knows *The Starry Night* is by Vincent van Gogh. Easy! But you spot three pictures that could be it...

Clue One, Part Two:

Look very hard, because
I'm hidden out of sight.
I will only be revealed,
on The Starry Night.

Which is the correct painting?

A

GO TO PAGE 19

B

FLIP TO PAGE 27

C

TURN TO PAGE 37

11

No, this is a Cubist painting. You can see more than one angle of each object.

TURN TO PAGE 16 AND **HAVE ANOTHER GO**

 No, Alexander Calder produced **Kinetic Art**.

TURN BACK TO PAGE 9 AND **HAVE ANOTHER GO**

 No. Although artists might feel relief when they finish a painting, it's not called a **relief**!

GO BACK TO PAGE 42 AND **GIVE YOURSELF ANOTHER CHANCE**

 No, not this time. The chandelier is actually a special piece of art, made with something more unusual than crystals.

TURN BACK TO PAGE 8 AND **THINK AGAIN**

 No, a red triangle is not right.

GO BACK TO PAGE 40 AND **TRY AGAIN**

Well done! The painting of cakes is by Wayne Thiebaud, who paints everyday things in bright colours.

You look behind the painting and sure enough, there's another envelope with a note inside.

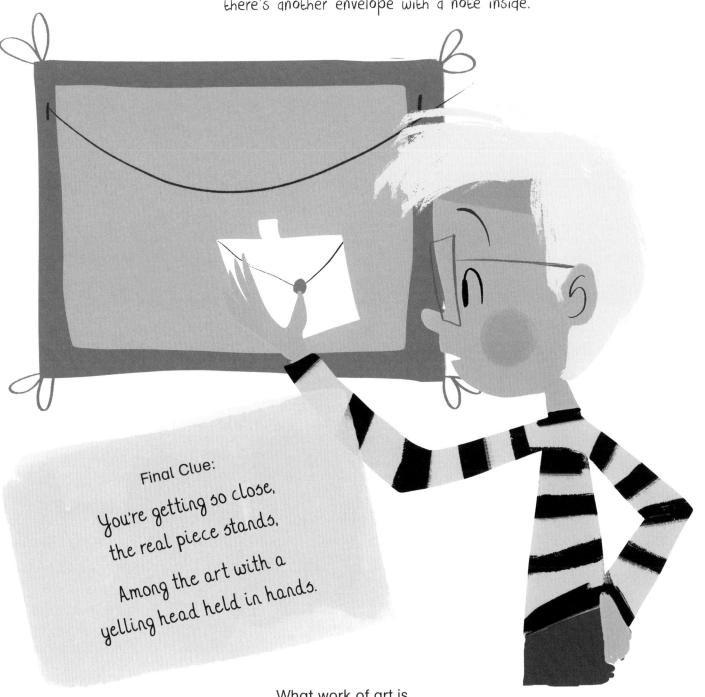

Final Clue:

You're getting so close,
the real piece stands,

Among the art with a
yelling head held in hands.

What work of art is
the riddle referring to?

EDVARD MUNCH'S
THE SCREAM.

TURN TO PAGE 24

VINCENT VAN GOGH'S
SORROWING OLD MAN.

FLIP TO PAGE 28

**LUCIAN FREUD'S *LEIGH
ON A GREEN SOFA.***

JUMP TO PAGE 33

Edvard Munch,
The Scream, 1893

£10,000

The judges hand you the trophy and a cheque for £10,000.
Cedric is beaming and promises a big celebration dinner
tonight - as well as a job at the gallery! Well done!

Well done! Andy Warhol is a famous American Pop Art artist.

ANDY WARHOL

You write a new, clear label and stick it over the smudged one, then take another look in the diary.

Put the two Cubist paintings (in brown frames) on the far wall of the exhibition room.

 You look around. There are three paintings in brown frames. Which is not a Cubist painting?

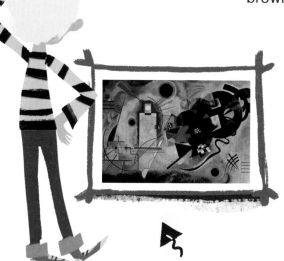

***YELLOW-RED-BLUE,
BY WASSILY KANDINSKY.***
TURN TO PAGE 31

***FACTORY, HORTA DE
EBRO,* BY PABLO PICASSO.**
FLIP TO PAGE 26

***THE GUITAR,*
BY JUAN GRIS.**
GO TO PAGE 12

 B That's not right.

**HAVE ANOTHER
LOOK** ON PAGE 28

 ! No, Don has nothing to do with it.

GO BACK
TO PAGE 10

Correct, it's all art! The bottles and confetti are an **installation** by Goldschmied & Chiari called *We Were Going to Dance Tonight*, the bricks are called *Equivalent VIII* by Carl Andre and the bronze bin bag is called *Trash* by Gavin Turk. Leave it all where it is!

Just then, Don and some men arrive carrying the Jackson Pollock painting you asked for earlier. They mount it on the wall. Don asks you:

Are you using art from that German movement of the early 20th century? What's it called?

You don't want to look stupid in front of Cedric's friend. What do you say?

 IT'S CALLED FUTURISM.
LOOK ON PAGE 30

 THE MOVEMENT YOU'RE THINKING OF IS SYMBOLISM.
TURN TO PAGE 37

 YOU'RE REFERRING TO EXPRESSIONISM.
GO TO PAGE 40

1 Yes! This certainly looks like the real *The Scream* that Edvard Munch created in 1893.

You try to remember which materials Edvard Munch used to check that this painting is real. You don't want to put up a children's painting!

Which materials should you be looking for?

OIL ON CANVAS.
TURN TO PAGE 8

WATERCOLOUR AND PASTELS ON PAPER.
GO TO PAGE 38

TEMPERA, OIL PAINTS AND PASTELS ON CARDBOARD.
OVER TO PAGE 5

 No, a **print** is flat, but a relief is not.

TURN BACK TO PAGE 42 AND **TRY AGAIN**

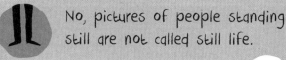 No, pictures of people standing still are not called still life.

TURN BACK TO PAGE 21 AND **THINK AGAIN**

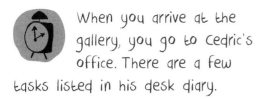 When you arrive at the gallery, you go to Cedric's office. There are a few tasks listed in his desk diary.

8:15 - Delivery of 'weather installation'
020 4907 4599
ParcelPronto

There have been no deliveries, so you phone ParcelPronto. There's been a mix-up and they're not sure which order is yours!

Which materials are needed for your installation?

 A LORRY FULL OF LIGHTS, FOIL AND HAZE MACHINES.
TURN TO PAGE 38

 UMBRELLAS AND SUNSHADES FOR THE JUDGES.
FLIP TO PAGE 21

 A PAINTING OF THE SUN.
JUMP TO PAGE 10

 No, *The Flame* is the right way up.

HAVE ANOTHER GO
ON PAGE 32

 Almost! This picture is by Vincent van Gogh but it's called *Starry Night over the Rhone*.

TRY AGAIN
ON PAGE 11

C

Correct! This is *Red Balloon*, painted by Paul Klee in 1922. The tell-tale signs of Naïve Art are when you first look, it seems like a child's painting, but after looking for longer, you can see more grown-up ideas and methods.

You order the painting and ask Daisy the receptionist to put it in the main exhibition room when it arrives.

MANAGER TO RECEPTION!

That's you! You rush to reception
ON PAGE 33

No, Laura Ford did not create this statue.

GO BACK TO PAGE 37 AND
HAVE ANOTHER TRY

Oh no! René Magritte is famous for his Surrealist style. This isn't a bold, commercial-style Pop Art painting.

HAVE ANOTHER TRY
ON PAGE 41 BEFORE THE JUDGES MARK YOU DOWN

 No, that's a kind thought, but the judges will be inside most of the time.

GO BACK TO PAGE 19 AND **TRY AGAIN**

 Yes, that's right! *The Massachusetts Chandelier* by Pipilotti Rist is an installation made out of underpants.

The judges smile as you show them the installation. You seem to be scraping through this!

Excellent. How unusual! Now, take us to the still life area, please.

Where do you take them?

TO THE PAINTINGS SHOWING EVERYDAY OBJECTS.
FLIP TO PAGE 9

TO THE AREA WHERE THERE ARE PICTURES OF PEOPLE STANDING STILL.
LOOK ON PAGE 18

TO THE SCULPTURE AREA.
TURN TO PAGE 36

 No, Edvard Munch always signed on the front, in the bottom left corner.

GO BACK TO PAGE 39 AND **TRY AGAIN**

Well done, Pointillism describes art that's made up of thousands of tiny coloured dots. Georges Seurat and Paul Signac were famous Pointillists. You get ready to reveal your showstopping piece...

Georges Seurat,
A Sunday on La Grande Jatte, 1884

Everyone is looking at you as you pull the curtain rope. There's a gasp in the room.

We're ready to see your most important work of art. We've been told it's very special!

Remarkable! I can hardly believe you've been allowed to borrow this work!

Why is it so special?

What do you say?

IT TOOK EDVARD MUNCH 50 YEARS TO PAINT.
TURN TO PAGE 27

IT'S THE ONLY ONE OF ITS KIND.
GO TO PAGE 23

IT WAS STOLEN IN THE PAST.
CHECK ON PAGE 39

22

No, Andy Garfield is an actor, most famous for the Spiderman movies.

TRY AGAIN ON PAGE 38

Andy Garfield, 2015

Edvard Munch,
The Scream, 1893

 Wrong! The painting of fruit is by Paul Cézanne, a famous Post-Impressionist.

CHECK AGAIN ON PAGE 7

 No, Edvard Munch actually made four versions of *The Scream*.

TURN BACK TO PAGE 22 AND **TRY AGAIN**

Yes! *The Scream* by Edvard Munch is the famous piece you're searching for. The gallery has a special display of *The Scream* by the local children.

You search among the art, but there are no more envelopes. But wait a minute – are they all painted by children? Some look suspiciously real...

1

2

3

Maybe one of these paintings is the real one,
hidden in plain sight! How ingenious of Cedric!

Which one could it be?

1 CHECK ON PAGE 18

2 GO TO PAGE 38 TO FIND OUT

3 TURN TO PAGE 43 TO SEE

B Correct! Jack the Dripper was the nickname given to the **Abstract Expressionist** Jackson Pollock, who dripped and threw paint onto huge canvases on the floor.

Portrait of Jackson Pollock in his studio, 1949

No, Kazimir Malevich didn't paint a purple circle.

HAVE ANOTHER GO ON PAGE 40

It seems strange that Cedric didn't mention Don, but you're sure the painting will be impressive. Don says he'll bring the painting over this afternoon, then leaves.

You receive a text message from Cedric.

Wrong – this is a Cubist painting. The artist has painted a picture from several points of view.

GO BACK TO PAGE 16 AND **TRY AGAIN**

○ ○ ○ ○　　2:07pm　　88%

< Messages　　　　Details >

Cedric

Forgot to say, can you pick a piece of Naïve Art from www.topartsite.com and get it delivered in an hour? Thanks.

SEND

 No, Jonathan Borofsky was not a blacksmith.

TRY AGAIN ON PAGE 29

No, it didn't take Edvard Munch that long!

GO BACK TO PAGE 22 AND **HAVE ANOTHER TRY**

No, that's *Nocturne in Black and Gold, the Falling Rocket* by James Abbott McNeill Whistler.

GO BACK TO PAGE 11 AND **TRY AGAIN** C

On the website, there's no 'naïve' option to choose from, so you'll have to work it out for yourself. You look at the Modern Art page, where there are only three artworks to choose from.

Which do you order?

Robert Delaunay, *Rythme, Joie de Vivre*, 1930

Paul Klee, *Red Balloon*, 1922

Edward Hopper, *House by the Railroad*, 1925

TURN TO PAGE 5

GO TO PAGE 20

JUMP TO PAGE 36

Yes, Kazuo Shiraga's art was as much about him performing with his feet as the paintings he produced.

So the clue is below your feet? The basement! You make your way down the rickety stairs towards the storage room.

Outside the room is a hi-tech door lock with three pictures.

You'll need to unjumble the pieces to enter the room. Which is the correct arrangement?

A
GO TO PAGE 31

B
TURN TO PAGE 16

C
LOOK ON PAGE 11

No, don't throw anything away! It could be modern art!

THINK AGAIN ON PAGE 35

No, *Sorrowing Old Man* by Vincent van Gogh doesn't show anyone yelling.

TRY AGAIN ON PAGE 13

Vincent van Gogh, *Sorrowing Old Man (At Eternity's Gate)*, 1890

The judges are in reception, being interviewed by a journalist. You notice Don watching. He's probably hoping you'll slip up!

You nervously introduce yourself and lead them to the main exhibition room.

Through the window is a giant sculpture of a hammering man.

Impressive! Can you tell us more about it?

This is your chance to make a good first impression.

What do you tell them?

JONATHAN BOROFSKY CREATED THIS IN 1979. IT MAKES HAMMERING NOISES.
FLIP TO PAGE 10

JONATHAN BOROFSKY CREATED THIS IN 1897. HE MADE IT USING HUNDREDS OF TINY HAMMERS.
TURN TO PAGE 39

JONATHAN BOROFSKY WAS A BLACKSMITH AND NAMED THE SCULPTURE AFTER HIMSELF.
TURN TO PAGE 26

That's correct. It's such a delicate work of art that no one has dared clean it, so it's actually quite grubby.

The judges start chatting to each other quietly and the journalist is taking pictures. Don looks like he might cry!

But what's that commotion outside the room?

TURN TO PAGE 14 TO **FIND OUT**

Munch, *m*, 1893

 Try again; a horse wasn't Laura Ford's focus.

TURN BACK TO PAGE 37 AND **HAVE ANOTHER GO**

 No, Futurism was practised by Italian artists.

GO BACK TO PAGE 17 AND **TRY ONCE MORE**

Well done! This is an **Abstract** painting. It's about colours and shapes, so it is not **Cubism**. Cubism is an **art movement** that tries to make objects look **3D** on a flat canvas.

You put the two Cubist works next to the door, ready to take with you later. The door opens and a head pokes around.

Hi! I'm Don. I own the gallery around the corner. Cedric and I are best friends and I said I'd lend him a masterpiece from my gallery. Would you like a painting by Derek the Dauber, Jack the Dripper or Fred the Engraver?

He's testing your knowledge.

Which do you choose?

DEREK THE DAUBER.
TURN TO PAGE 8 **A**

JACK THE DRIPPER.
LOOK ON PAGE 26 **B**

FRED THE ENGRAVER.
GO TO PAGE 43 **C**

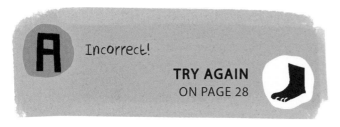 Incorrect!

TRY AGAIN
ON PAGE 28

 The expressive, freely painted *Charing Cross Bridge* by André Derain is a **Fauvist** painting, not Pop Art.

TRY AGAIN ON
PAGE 41 QUICKLY

Yes! Performance Art keeps things fun. Artists like Mark Wallinger and Nick Cave often wear costumes and perform in art galleries.

The judges look delighted as they've never seen anything like it before. Feeling more relaxed, you take them towards the far wall.

Jackson Pollock, *The Flame*, 1938

Georg Baselitz, *Adieu*, 1982

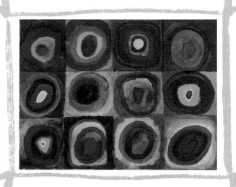

Wassily Kandinsky,
*Squares with
Concentric Circles*, 1913

Stop!

One of those paintings is upside down! We can't allow such mistakes!

Oh no! You'll need to fix it quickly.

Which one is upside down?

THE FLAME BY JACKSON POLLOCK.
FLIP TO PAGE 19

SQUARES WITH CONCENTRIC CIRCLES BY WASSILY KANDINSKY.
TURN TO PAGE 41

ADIEU BY GEORG BASELITZ.
GO TO PAGE 10

Police officers are waiting for you at reception. They explain that they've been given a tip-off that there is a forged Lucian Freud painting at this gallery. You take them to the Freud painting.

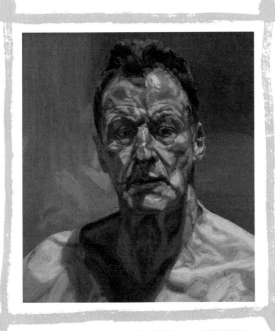

Lucian Freud, *Reflection (Self-Portrait)*, 1985

How can you be sure that this is a painting by Lucian Freud and not a forgery?

What is typical of a Freud painting?

IT'S PAINTED IN BRILLIANT COLOURS.
TURN TO PAGE 39

THE PAINTING IS OUTLINED IN BLACK.
GO TO PAGE 9

IT'S PAINTED WITH THICK PAINT.
GO TO PAGE 42

 No, *Leigh on a Green Sofa*, by Lucian Freud, shows the model posing with his head on his hands, not in them!

TRY AGAIN
ON PAGE 13

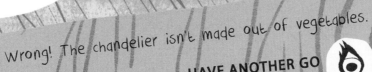

 Wrong! The chandelier isn't made out of vegetables.

HAVE ANOTHER GO
ON PAGE 8

Top marks! You tell Daisy to look in the office for raised 3D pictures or designs. She looks relieved!

It's time to check the main exhibition room, which is closed to the public while it's being prepared for the judges to arrive. When you get there, you see it's filled with empty bottles, rubbish bags and bricks!

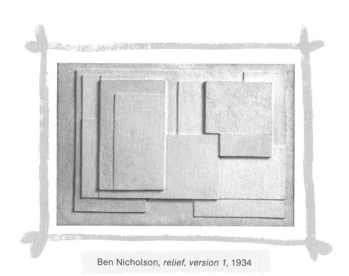

Ben Nicholson, *relief, version 1*, 1934

The caretaker's clearing up and he calls you over.

Some idiot has left this rubbish here. Shall I clear it all away?

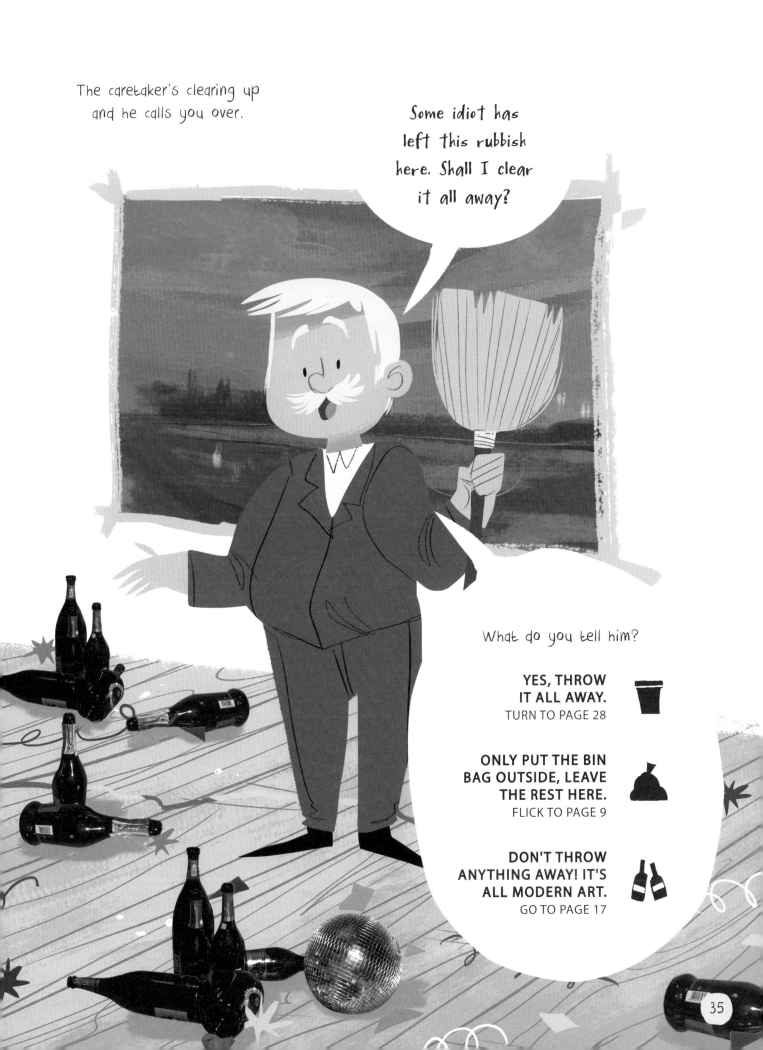

What do you tell him?

YES, THROW IT ALL AWAY.
TURN TO PAGE 28

ONLY PUT THE BIN BAG OUTSIDE, LEAVE THE REST HERE.
FLICK TO PAGE 9

DON'T THROW ANYTHING AWAY! IT'S ALL MODERN ART.
GO TO PAGE 17

Yes, Kazimir Malevich's *Black Square*, painted in 1913, was the first work of art that didn't try to represent anything from the real world.

Using the password **SQUARE**, you open the safe and take out a note.

Kazimir Malevich, *Black Square*, 1913

The highly prized work of art for this year's exhibition is carefully hidden. Solve the clues to find it.

Clue One, Part One:

To find this precious piece,
you must look high and low.
Below Shiraga's painting tool,
is where you must go.

Clue One, Part Two:

Look very hard, because
I'm hidden out of sight.
I will only be revealed,
on The Starry Night.

 No, although sculpture is usually still, it's not called still life.

HAVE ANOTHER GO ON PAGE 21

Firstly, what did Shiraga paint with?

HIS HANDS.
CHECK ON PAGE 42

HIS MOUTH.
GO TO PAGE 5

HIS FEET.
LOOK ON PAGE 28

Wrong! This is *House by the Railroad*, painted in 1925 by Edward Hopper who was an American Realist.

TRY AGAIN ON PAGE 27 **B**

Yes, that's Vincent van Gogh's *The Starry Night!* You carefully pick up the painting, and feel for the envelope stuck on the back, revealing the second clue.

Vincent van Gogh,
The Starry Night, 1889

Clue Two:

To find my hiding place, you must select Laura Ford's masterpiece – which one is correct?

Which one is by Laura Ford?

 GO TO PAGE 6

 TURN TO PAGE 20

 FLICK TO PAGE 30

No, Symbolism was produced mainly in France at the end of the 19th century.

TURN BACK TO PAGE 17 AND **LOOK AGAIN**

No, Bridget Riley's art is called **Op Art**, not Pointillism.

GO BACK TO PAGE 9 AND **TRY AGAIN**

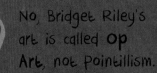

Yes, that's right! In 2003, Olafur Eliasson made a huge installation called *The Weather Project* that featured a pretend sun, mist and other weather effects.

You tell the company to deliver Olafur Eliasson's equipment as soon as possible and take another look at the diary.

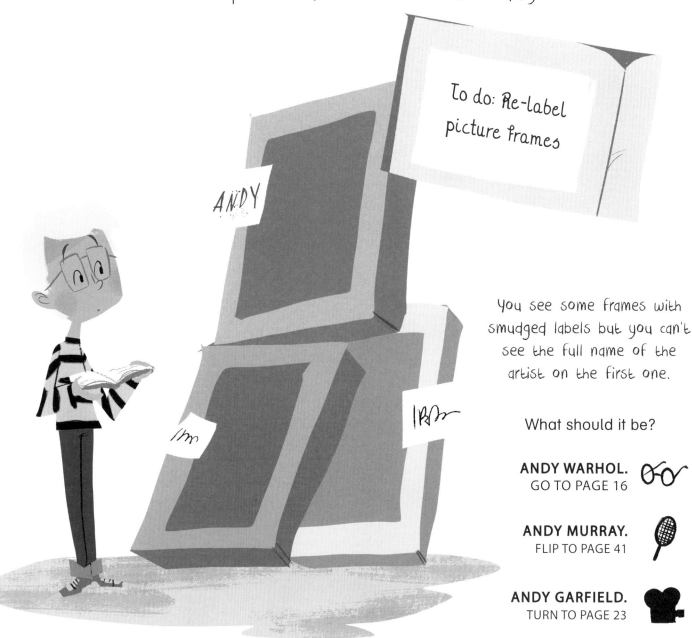

To do: Re-label picture frames

ANDY

You see some frames with smudged labels but you can't see the full name of the artist on the first one.

What should it be?

ANDY WARHOL.
GO TO PAGE 16

ANDY MURRAY.
FLIP TO PAGE 41

ANDY GARFIELD.
TURN TO PAGE 23

 No, *The Scream* was not made with watercolour on paper.

RETURN TO PAGE 18 AND CHOOSE A DIFFERENT MATERIAL **1**

2 No, there's only one figure in the background of this work. Edvard Munch's painting has two.

GO BACK TO PAGE 25 AND **HAVE ANOTHER GO**

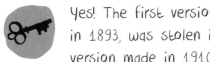
Yes! The first version of *The Scream*, made in 1893, was stolen in 1994, and another version made in 1910 was stolen in 2004. The Norwegian government is extremely wary of letting it out of their sight! Don exclaims...

You would never have been allowed to exhibit this painting! How do you know it isn't a fake?

What do you tell him?

IT'S ON DELICATE CARDBOARD, AND AS IT HASN'T BEEN CLEANED FOR YEARS, IT'S DIRTY.
GO TO PAGE 30

IT'S SIGNED ON THE BACK AS EDVARD MUNCH ALWAYS DID.
TURN TO PAGE 21

ALTHOUGH IT LOOKS SKETCHY, IT'S ACTUALLY PAINTED IN EDVARD MUNCH'S PAINSTAKING STYLE.
TURN TO PAGE 43

✗ No, this was made in the late 20th century. It is made of metal or wood, with motors to make the arm appear to hammer.

TRY AGAIN
ON PAGE 29

 No, Lucian Freud painted with subdued colours.

GO BACK TO PAGE 33
AND **TRY AGAIN**

That's right, Expressionism was mainly a German art movement at the beginning of the 20th century.

Your mobile phone rings. It's Cedric, so you go into the office, closing the door behind you.

The main artwork for the exhibition will make the gallery internationally famous. It's hidden, so no one can steal it. Watch out for Don as he'll try to sabotage the exhibition.

Only a true art expert will find it. I'm hoping that's you! The first clue is in the office safe. The password is the shape of Kazimir Malevich's most famous painting.

Oh no! Cedric and Don aren't friends. There's the safe, but what's the password?

What's the shape of Kazimir Malevich's most famous painting?

A RED TRIANGLE.
TURN TO PAGE 12

A PURPLE CIRCLE.
LOOK ON PAGE 26

A BLACK SQUARE.
CHECK ON PAGE 36

Afraid not! Andy Murray is a British tennis player, not an artist.

TRY AGAIN ON PAGE 38

No, the soup can is a famous print by Andy Warhol.

RETURN TO PAGE 7 AND **LOOK AGAIN**

 Yes. You're not the first gallery to make a mistake. The Museum of Modern Art in New York also hung Henri Matisse's *Le Bateau* upside down in 1961! You quickly switch it the right way up.

André Derain, *Charing Cross Bridge*, 1906

Roy Lichtenstein, *Stepping Out*, 1978

René Magritte, *The Great War*, 1964

May I ask if you could tell me more about the Pop Art painting?

Which painting is she talking about?

***THE GREAT WAR* BY RENÉ MAGRITTE.**
CHECK ON PAGE 20

***STEPPING OUT* BY ROY LICHTENSTEIN.**
TURN TO PAGE 8

***CHARING CROSS BRIDGE* BY ANDRÉ DERAIN.**
LOOK ON PAGE 31

41

Correct! Lucian Freud painted with thick paint, known as **impasto**.

The police officers take some notes and leave. Daisy comes dashing towards you, looking troubled.

Can you help me? Cedric asked me to put the relief on the reception wall. But what's a relief?

What do you tell her?

IT'S A FINISHED PAINTING.
TURN TO PAGE 12

IT'S A PRINT.
GO TO PAGE 18

IT'S A 3D PICTURE DESIGN.
FLIP TO PAGE 34

 No, Kazuo Shiraga didn't famously paint with his hands.

GO BACK TO PAGE 36 AND **TRY AGAIN**

 No, the person wearing a costume is not performing at a children's party.

GO BACK TO PAGE 10 AND **TRY AGAIN**

C Wrong! Fred the Engraver is not a famous artist.

TURN BACK TO PAGE 31 AND **HAVE ANOTHER GO**

3 No, the head's too big and the fence next to him is fancier than in the real painting.

TURN BACK TO PAGE 25 AND **TRY AGAIN**

 It looks sketchy because it is! Edvard Munch made it quickly and expressively, not slowly and carefully.

RETURN TO PAGE 39 AND **HAVE ANOTHER GO**

GLOSSARY

2D
Short for two-dimensional, meaning flat, such as a square.

3D
Short for three-dimensional, meaning solid, such as a cube.

Abstract Art
Art with no recognizable things in it from the real world.

Abstract Expressionism
Expressive, usually abstract, painting from the 1940s, '50s and '60s.

Action painting
A method of painting in which artists drip, splatter or throw paint at their canvases. It began as part of Abstract Expressionism.

Art movement
A type or style of art that happens at a particular time. Some are planned by artists, whereas others are named later by other people.

Avant-garde art
Art that is new and original, and introduces different ideas.

Bronze
A metal made by combining copper and tin, often used in sculpture.

Cubism
A movement that started in 1907 where artists tried to show the 3D world on 2D surfaces, with several viewpoints at once.

Expressionism
Art that expresses feelings, usually through exaggerated or distorted pictures, colours and shapes.

Fauvism
Beginning in 1905, a group of artists who painted in bright colours to express feelings.

Figurative Art
Also called Representational Art, it shows things that are recognizable from the real world.

Fine Art
Art made for itself, not for any practical purpose, including paintings, sculpture, installations, drawings and prints.

Futurism
An Italian art movement before World War II that celebrated machines, speed, technology and cities.

Impasto
Paint that is applied thickly.

Impressionism
A late 19th-century art movement that focused on painting moments in time with quick, short brushmarks and bright colours.

Installation
Huge mixed media constructions, designed to be displayed in certain places for short times.

Kinetic Art
Works of art that move, such as the mobiles by Alexander Calder.

GLOSSARY

Naive Art
Often detailed and bright paintings, without **perspective**, usually by artists who did not train at art school.

Neo-Impressionism
Late 19th-century French movement, building on **Impressionism** with bright colours and Pointillism.

Op Art
Short for 'Optical art', it features lines and shapes that have various effects on viewers' eyes.

Orphism
Inspired by Cubism, a French art movement using colour and abstract shapes that are harmonious, like music.

Pastels
Chalk pastels are chalky, coloured sticks; oil pastels are waxy, coloured sticks.

Perspective
Ways of showing depth and distance on 2D surfaces.

Pigment
Powdered colours that are mixed with different substances to make art materials such as paint and coloured pencils.

Pointillism
A style of painting with pictures made of tiny dots of pure, unmixed colours.

Pop Art
Art movement from the 1950s and '60s, mainly in London and New York, that used popular images inspired by advertising, films and magazines.

Print
An image made by taking an impression from something else. Artists make several types of print, including etching, lino cuts and screenprints.

Relief
An image with a raised surface.

Still life
Objects that do not move; arrangements for paintings, photography and sculpture.

Suprematism
Developed by Kazimir Malevich in 1915 in Russia, an art movement using only geometric shapes and flat-looking colours.

Surrealism
A 20th-century art movement which explored dreams and fantasy worlds.

Symbolism
Including symbols in art to show ideas; and also a 19th-century art and literary movement that was about ideas, thoughts and dreams, but not reality.

Tempera
Used since ancient times, paint made from mixing dry pigment with egg yolk. It lost popularity among painters when oil paints were made.

Watercolour
See-through (transparent) paint that has to be mixed with water.

ARTIST INDEX

Carl Andre (born 1935)
American Minimalist sculptor.

Georg Baselitz (born 1938)
German painter, draughtsman, printmaker and sculptor who creates expressive, **Figurative Art.**

Jonathan Borofsky (born 1942)
American sculptor and printmaker who tries to link life and art more closely.

Alexander Calder (1898-1976)
American Kinetic artist who produced the first **Fine Art** mobile.

Paul Cezanne (1839-1906)
French painter who worked with the Impressionists, then invented his own way of painting, which helped to inspire Cubism.

Robert Delaunay (1885-1941)
French painter who developed Orphism, influenced by Cubism, focusing on colour, shapes and rhythm.

Andre Derain (1880-1954)
French painter who was involved with Fauvism and Cubism.

Olafur Eliasson (born 1967)
Danish-Icelandic artist producing sculpture and installations using things such as light and water.

Laura Ford (born 1961)
British sculptor who creates mainly figurative works, often animals.

Lucian Freud (1922-2011)
British painter, who painted many expressive portraits, mainly of people he knew.

Vincent van Gogh (1853-1890)
Dutch artist, linked with Post-Impressionism, famous for his short life and the high price of his paintings since his death.

Goldschmied & Chiari, or Sara Goldschmied (born 1975) and Eleonora Chiari (born 1971)
Italian artists who create installations, videos and photography, exploring ideas about memory.

Juan Gris (1887-1927)
Spanish Cubist painter and sculptor.

Edward Hopper (1882-1967)
American painter of realistic landscapes and seemingly lonely people.

Wassily Kandinsky (1866-1944)
Russian painter and one of the first abstract artists.

Paul Klee (1879-1940)
Swiss-German artist influenced by Expressionism, Cubism and Surrealism.

Roy Lichtenstein (1923-1997)
American Pop Art painter and sculptor who made cartoons into Fine Art.

Kazimir Malevich (1878-1935)
Russian painter who invented **Suprematism** in 1915.

Henri Matisse (1869-1954)
French painter and sculptor who became the leader of Fauvism.

Joan Miró (1893-1983)
Spanish Surrealist painter who used abstract elements in his work.

Claude Monet (1840-1926)
French Impressionist who painted changing effects of natural light.

Edvard Munch (1863-1944)
Norwegian painter influenced by Vincent van Gogh, whose emotional paintings inspired Expressionism.

Jackson Pollock (1912-1956)
American Abstract Expressionist who invented **action painting**, also known as drip painting.

Bridget Riley (born 1931)
British Op Art painter who creates large paintings with lines and shapes that seem to move or change colour.

Pipilotti Rist (born 1962)
Swiss artist who creates videos, film and installations using light and colour.

Kazuo Shiraga (1924-2008)
Japanese **avant-garde** abstract painter.

Paul Signac (1863-1935)
French **Neo-Impressionist** who helped to invent Pointillism.

Wayne Thiebaud (born 1920)
American artist linked with Pop Art who paints ordinary things such as pies, lipsticks and cakes.

Andy Warhol (1928-1987)
American Pop Art artist who created art from advertising and the media.

James Abbott McNeill Whistler (1834-1903)
American-born, British-based artist whose paintings focused on harmony and helped to inspire Abstract Art.

TAKING IT FURTHER

The Art Quest books are designed to inspire children to develop and apply their artistic understanding and knowledge about art and artists through compelling adventure stories. For each story, readers must solve a series of problems and challenges on their way to completing an exciting quest.

The books do not follow a page-by-page pattern. Instead, the reader jumps forwards and backwards through the book according to the answers he or she gives to the problems. If the answers are correct, the reader progresses to the next stage of the story; incorrect answers are fully explained before the reader is directed back to attempt the problem once again.

Additional help may be found in the glossary on **pages 44 to 45**.

TO HELP YOUR CHILD DEVELOP THEIR UNDERSTANDING OF ART, YOU CAN:

- Read the book with your child.

- Continue reading with your child until they understand how to follow the 'Go to' instructions to the next puzzle or explanation and is flipping through the book confidently.

- Encourage your child to read on alone. Prompt them to tell you how the story develops and what problems they have solved.

- Ask your child what they think of art. Do they like paintings or sculpture best? Which art is their favourite and why? What do they think the world would be like with no artists?

- Discuss with your child what it might be like if they had their own gallery. What art would they have there? What would visitors want to see? How difficult is it to make art?

- Take advantage of galleries, museums, books and websites that contain information about art. Be careful to only go to respected websites or the information may not be accurate. These resources — many specially for children — can provide plenty of further information that can show your child a lot more about art — both practical and art history.

- Remember, we all learn best when we are enjoying ourselves, so encourage your child to have fun when learning about art!